The Electric Strength Of Air, Part 4

John Boswell Whitehead

In the interest of creating a more extensive selection of rare historical book reprints, we have chosen to reproduce this title even though it may possibly have occasional imperfections such as missing and blurred pages, missing text, poor pictures, markings, dark backgrounds and other reproduction issues beyond our control. Because this work is culturally important, we have made it available as a part of our commitment to protecting, preserving and promoting the world's literature. Thank you for your understanding.

A paper to be presented at the 30th Annual Convention of the American Institute of Electrical Engineers, Cooperstown, N.Y., June 27, 1913.

Copyright, 1913. By A. I. E. E.
(*Subject to final revision for the Transactions.*)

THE ELECTRIC STRENGTH OF AIR—IV

BY J. B. WHITEHEAD AND T. T. FITCH

I. INTRODUCTION

This paper describes the results of a series of investigations on the effects of pressure, temperature and density of gas upon the formation of the corona in air. It is largely an extension of work described in the second of this series of papers.

The study of the influence of temperature and pressure on corona-forming voltage was begun by Ryan in 1904. The influence of pressure in its relation to the size of conductor was shown in the second of this series of papers. The influence of temperature and pressure has been investigated also by Peek who has given an interesting empirical formula connecting critical corona intensity in air with pressure, temperature and size of conductor. The influence of pressure on critical corona intensity has been studied by Watson for the case of continuous voltage. The purpose of the present work has been the extension of the earlier investigations both as to range of pressure and size of conductor and also to obtain further information on the influence of temperature. Some observations were also made with carbon dioxide as the gas surrounding the conductor instead of air to see what part, if any, is played by the density of the gas.

The larger part of the work is the study of variation of critical or corona-forming intensity with pressure. For this work conductors varying from 0.438 to 0.950 cm. in diameter were used, and the pressure was varied from 5 to 110 cm. of mercury.

II. REVIEW OF EARLIER WORK ON PRESSURE AND TEMPERATURE

A brief review of earlier investigations on the variation of critical intensity with pressure and temperature will not be out of place. Some other points, also, have such an intimate relation to these variations or at least to a study of them that they will be mentioned.

It was shown by Ryan[1] that for the one size of conductor which he used the critical intensity is a linear function of the pressure from 40 to 90 cm. of mercury. A similar relation was shown to hold for variations with temperature between 21 and 93 deg. cent.

Watson published a set of experiments[2] in 1909 showing a linear relation between pressure and critical intensity for the case of continuous voltage. His range of pressure was from 36 to 76 cm. of mercury and of size of conductor from 0.07 to 0.95 cm. He also gave curves showing the amount of current passing.

In the earlier papers of this series numerous curves were given showing a linear relation between critical intensity and pressure from 38 to 100 cm. The conductors used ranged in diameter from 0.122 to 0.475 cm. Some experiments were also made showing a linear relation between critical intensity and temperature. Only one size of conductor was used. The range of temperature was from 8 to 41 deg. cent.

It has further been shown in these papers that:

The critical intensity is independent of free ionization, moisture content and velocity of the air.

The visual critical intensity is identical with that determined by an electroscope.

The critical intensity g for clean round conductors for a pressure of 76 cm. and temperature of 20 degrees may be expressed by the formula:

$$g = A + \frac{B}{\sqrt{D}} \qquad (1)$$

where A and B are constants and D is the diameter of the conductor. This formula is discussed in a later paragraph.

Peek[3] has given the results of a set of experiments on the variation of critical intensity with temperature showing practically a linear law between -20 and $+140$ deg. cent. He has also given a general formula covering the variations of critical

---

1. Ryan: *Conductivity of the Atmosphere at High Voltages*, TRANS. A. I. E. E., Vol. XXIII, 1904.
2. *Electrician*, Vol. LXIII, 1909.
3. Peek: *The Law of Corona*, TRANS. A. I. E. E., Vol. XXXI, 1912.

intensity with change of temperature and pressure for a tube and concentric conductor as follows:

$$g = 31\, \delta \left(1 + \frac{0.308}{\sqrt{\delta\, r}}\right) \qquad (2)$$

where g is the critical intensity in kilovolts per cm., r is the radius of conductor and

$$\delta = \frac{3.92\, p}{273 + t}$$

p being the pressure in cm. of mercury and t the temperature centigrade. So far as we can find the only statements he has given concerning the influence of pressure on the variation of critical intensity are a curve[4] giving observations on a 2.54-cm. conductor for pressures from 2 to 65 cm. and a table of values of δ and corresponding values of g in closing the discussion of his 1912 paper.[5] No description of his methods was given.

III. Present Work

The observations which are recorded in this paper were made in the spring of 1912. They aim to supply, in part, the lack of sufficiently extensive data on variation of critical corona intensity with pressure and size of conductor.

Apparatus and Equipment. For the pressure measurements a 20-cm. iron tube about 90 cm. in length was used. The ends were fitted with insulating caps about 18 cm. long. These caps were made of impregnated fibre, and served the double purpose of insulation and sealing for the variation of air pressure both above and below that of the atmosphere. A rotary air pump permitted evacuation of the tube to about five cm. of mercury in five minutes. Most changes of pressure could be made in a minute or two, but owing to numerous joints necessary for insulation purposes there was present some leakage, which necessitated a longer time to exhaust to the lowest pressure reached, and set the limit of about five cm. as the minimum.

A small glass window was placed in the tube for making visual observations of the corona, but during most of the work the gold leaf electroscope was used for detecting the point at

---

4. Peek: "Nature of Corona," *Gen. Elec. Review*, December, 1912.
5. Peek: Proc. A. I. E. E., November, 1912.

which corona begins. This method has been described in detail in the first of these papers so no further description is necessary here. Fig. 1 shows the general arrangement of the apparatus. The beginning of corona is very sharply defined. A change of one per cent or less in the voltage will cause the time of complete discharge to change from about a half hour to five seconds. Any difference between the beginning of corona as observed by the eye and by the discharge of the electroscope is within this small error of observation.

The observations on the influence of temperature were made with a similar apparatus, except that the tube was in this case surrounded by a water jacket. Hand stirring of the water was found to be sufficient to keep the temperature of the air within the tube uniform to about two degrees. Only the smaller sizes of conductor could be used in this apparatus owing to spark-over troubles occasioned by the reduced size of outer tube. The heating was done by gas burners and ice was used for getting reduced temperature.

Source of Power. The power for all the experiments was drawn from a 10-kw., 100,000-volt transformer. The transformer was operated by a motor-generator set of 7.5 kw. capacity, the generator field being excited by a storage battery, resulting in good voltage control. All experiments were made at a frequency of 60 cycles. The transformer is provided with a

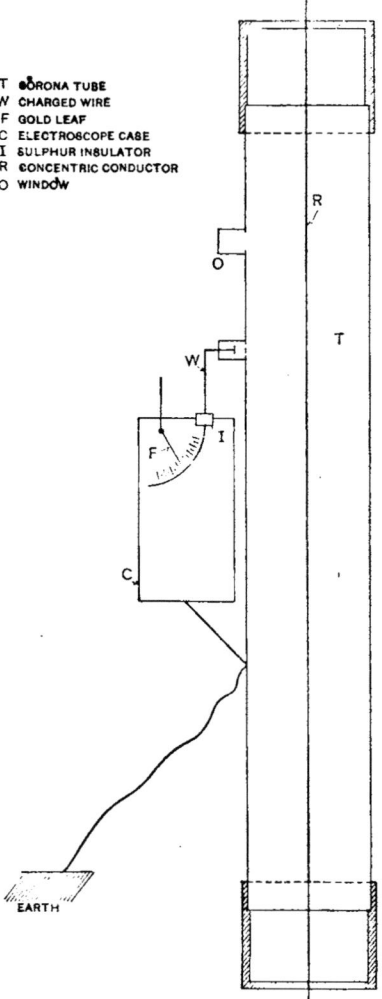

T CORONA TUBE
W CHARGED WIRE
F GOLD LEAF
C ELECTROSCOPE CASE
I SULPHUR INSULATOR
R CONCENTRIC CONDUCTOR
O WINDOW

Fig. 1.—Arrangement of Apparatus

test coil giving 120 volts for 100,000 volts on the high-tension terminals as computed from the ratio of primary and secondary turns. This test coil was used entirely in making measurements of the voltage. All determinations of ratio of maximum to mean effective voltage were also obtained from this coil.

Ratio of Maximum to Mean Effective Voltage. For the purpose of checking the results this ratio was determined by two methods. The first makes use of the oscillograph, the second of a rotating contactor and the principle of the potentiometer.

The ratio was determined from the oscillograms by reading a number of ordinates, usually about 30 or 40 to a cycle. From these ordinates taken at equal distances the ratio of maximum to the square root of the mean square value was computed. The principal difficulty with this method is to obtain an oscillogram with lines sufficiently sharp and narrow.

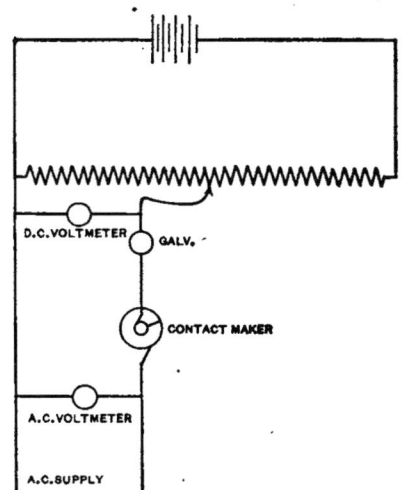

FIG. 2.—METHOD OF MEASURING RATIO OF MAXIMUM TO MEAN EFFECTIVE VOLTAGE

The contactor method is indicated in Fig. 2, the contact wheel being placed on the generator shaft. In the actual apparatus a handle was provided for readily shifting the point of contact. By reference to the galvanometer the contact can be shifted until the closure occurs on the peak of the wave. Then the slider on the rheostat is moved until the galvanometer indicates zero deflection. The readings of the continuous and alternating voltmeters are then taken. The ratio of their readings in volts is the ratio desired, the direct-current voltmeter indicating the maximum voltage and the alternating-current voltmeter the mean effective value.

The chief difficulty with this method is to keep the source of alternating voltage sufficiently steady during the time necessary for an observation. A damped galvanometer of fairly high sensibility is required. Only the relative calibration of the voltmeters is necessary since the ratio is all that is required. The alternating voltmeter used was of the electrodynamometer type and it was compared with the direct-current voltmeter by taking the mean of readings with reversed polarity.

Table I, of which Fig. 3 is a plot, gives the ratio of maximum to mean effective voltage for the various voltages on the test

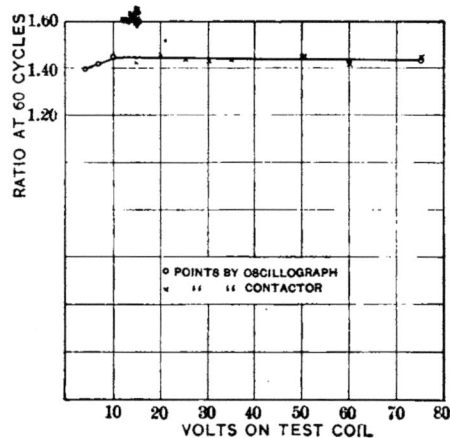

Fig. 3.—Ratio of Maximum to Mean Effective Volts. From Test Coil of 100,000-Volt Transformer

coil of the transformer used in the experiments. The values taken from the curve were used in making reductions of readings on critical intensity.

Fig. 4 is a reproduction from a typical oscillogram.

TABLE I

Test coil volts	Ratio = Max./Mean eff.		
	Contactor	Oscillograph	From curve
4		1.395	1.400
7		1.420	1.420
10		1.450	1.440
15	1.431		1.440
20	1.459		1.445
25	1.436		1.445
30	1.429		1.445
35	1.438		1.445
50	1.444	1.446	1.440
60	1.421	1.430	1.440
75	1.452	1.427	1.440

Variation of Critical Intensity with Gas Pressure. Fig. 5 shows the observed variation of critical corona voltage with pressure, while Fig. 6 shows the corresponding variation of critical intensity computed from the same observations. As mentioned before, nine conductors varying from 0.238 to 0.950 cm. in diameter were used. Above 30 or 40 cm. pressure the curves are nearly straight; the curvature being so slight as to be within the error of observation. They explain, therefore, the conclusion of the earlier paper that the relation between pressure and critical intensity is linear in this region.

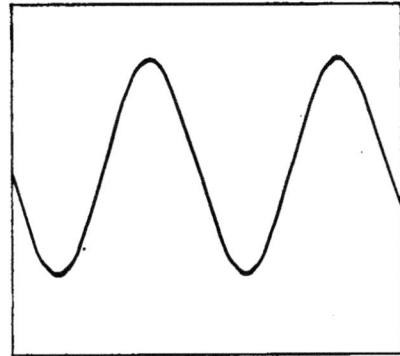

FIG. 4 —TAKEN AT 60 CYCLES AND 60 VOLTS

We have used the expression

$$\frac{dv}{dr} = \frac{E}{r \log \frac{R}{r}}$$

for calculating the critical intensity in kilovolts per cm. from the observed critical voltage on the transformer test coil. E is the maximum voltage on the conductor obtained by taking into account the ratio of transformation of the transformer, and the ratio of maximum to mean effective voltage, while r and R are the radii of conductor and tube, respectively.

Table II gives a typical set of observations.

Several readings were taken at each pressure as shown in the readings for the last three pressures. The pressure was determined by use of a gauge or monometer. This method gives, of course, only the difference of pressure between that in the tube

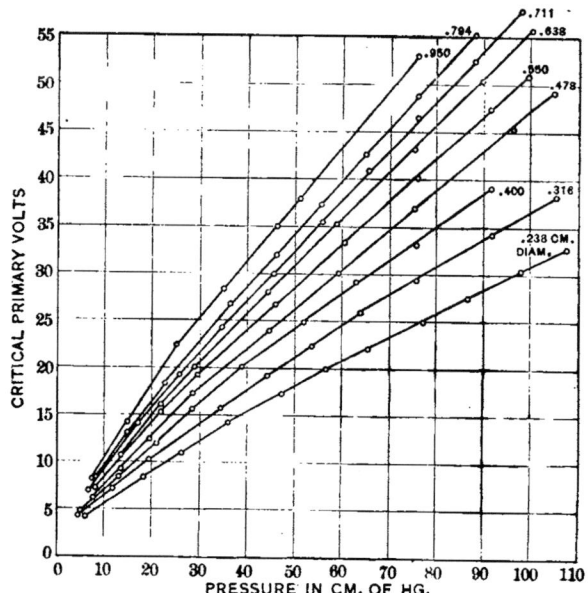

Fig 5.—Observed Variation of Critical Corona Voltage with Pressure. Transformer Ratio = 833

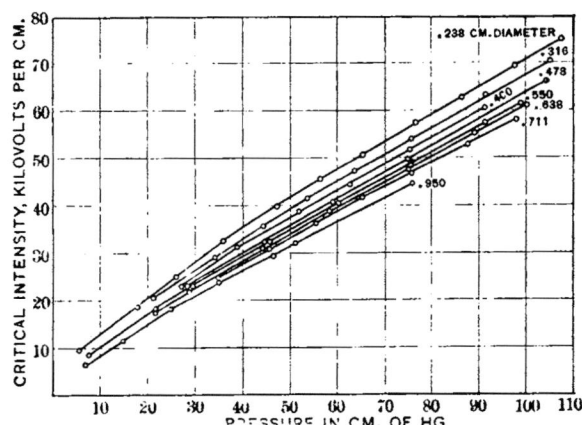

Fig. 6.—Variation of Critical Intensity with Pressure and Size of Conductor at 20 deg. cent.

and atmospheric. For this reason it was necessary to read the barometer to obtain the absolute pressure. The voltage was read by two Weston alternating-current voltmeters of suitable ranges connected to the test coil of the transformer, as stated. In taking readings the electroscope was first charged and then the voltage gradually raised till the electroscope was suddenly discharged, as shown by the fall of the gold leaf. Atten-

TABLE II

Diameter of conductor 0.316 cm.   Transformer ratio 833 $\dfrac{1}{r \log R/r} = 1.539$

Gauge readings mm. of hg.		Diff.	Temp. deg. cent	Barometer	Pressure mm.	Test coils volts	Ratio $\dfrac{\text{max.}}{\text{eff.}}$	Critical kilovolts max.	Critical intensity kv. cm.
288	1000	712	18.2	760	48	4.5	1.40	5.2	8.0
316	960	644	18.2	760	116	7.2	1.42	8.5	13.1
348	915	567	18.2	760	193	10.3	1.44	12.3	18.9
361	910	549	19.8	756	207	10.9	1.44	13.0	20.0
365	909	544	19.8	756	212	11.2	1.44	13.4	20.6
431	846	415	19.8	756	341	15.7	1.44	18.9	29.1
484	799	315	19.8	756	441	19.3	1.44	23.2	35.7
530	750	220	19.8	756	536	22.4	1.445	27.0	41.5
592	710	118	19.8	756	638	25.5	1.445	30.7	47.2
					756	29.3	1.445		
			19.8	756	756	29.5	1.445	35.5	54.6
					756	29.5			
					756	29.3			
755	597	158			914	34.0	1.445		
755	597	158			914	33.9			
754	597	157	19.8	756	913	34.0		41.0	63.1
754	597	157			913	33.9			
849	554	295			1051	38.2			
850	555	295	19.8	756	1051	38.2	1.445	46.0	70.8
850	555	295			1051	38.2			
850	555	295			1051	38.2			

tion is called to the accuracy with which observations may be repeated.

Empirical Formulas. As stated before, Peek has given the formula

$$g = 31\,\delta\left(1 + \frac{0.308}{\sqrt{\delta\,r}}\right)$$

connecting the critical intensity g in kilovolts per cm. with pressure, temperature and radius of conductor. Fig. 8 shows curves for three sizes of conductor for the temperature 20 deg. cent. As indicated, the circles are observed points while the full lines are plotted from the formula given above. It is seen that as the formula stands it does not meet our observations very closely, though it gives a curve of the correct general form. By suitable changes in the constants the formula is brought into close agreement.

Fig. 9 is plotted from the formula

$$g = 33.6\,\delta\left(1 + \frac{0.235}{\sqrt{\delta\,r}}\right) \qquad (2)$$

The circles show the observed points as before. It is seen that with the formula so changed it represents the observations about

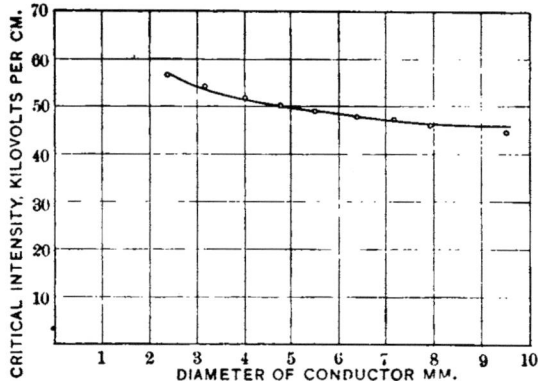

Fig. 7.—Variation of Critical Intensity with Size of Conductor at 20 deg. cent. and 76 cm. Pressure

as closely as the readings can be taken. This formula gives zero voltage for zero pressure provided r has a value greater than zero, which, of course, it has for any real case. As the present observations run only as low as 4 or 5 cm. pressure, they furnish no test on this point. Investigations are now under way to determine what becomes of the corona at very low pressures.

If in equation (2) the value of δ at 76 cm. pressure and temperature 20 deg. be substituted, the following formula is obtained:

$$g = 34 + \frac{11.2}{\sqrt{D}} \qquad (3)$$

This formula gives the variation of critical intensity with D the diameter of conductor at standard temperature and pressure.

The curve in Fig. 7 is a plot from this equation while the circles are observed points. In the earlier work a formula of the same form but with different constants was given, namely:

$$g = 32 + \frac{13.4}{\sqrt{D}} \qquad (4)$$

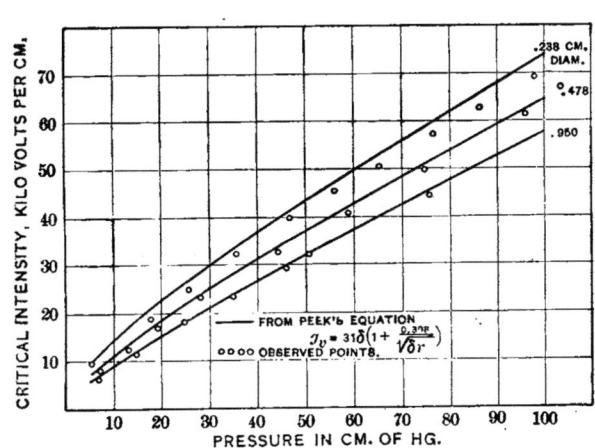

FIG. 8

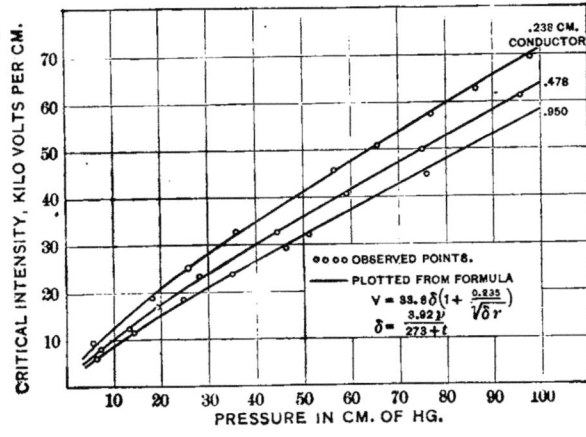

FIG. 9

The first constant of formula (4) is less than that of formula (3) while the second is greater, so the difference is largely one of curvature. What difference there is over the range of conductors observed is accounted for by a small discrepancy in the ratios of transformation of the transformers used in the earlier experiments and in the present ones. It was found by trial in the earlier experiments that the indicated critical voltage with the 30,000-volt transformer with which those experiments were conducted was 54 kv. for a 0.345-cm. conductor and 52.4 for the 100,000-volt transformer which was used in the present set of experiments. These two differing values were obtained at the same time and with voltage from the same generator. Allowing for this discrepancy the present observations are brought into close agreement with the older values. As the purpose of this work is the investigation of the influence of density of gas on critical corona intensity, and as the above discrepancy does not affect the results relatively, its elimination has been left to a later date.

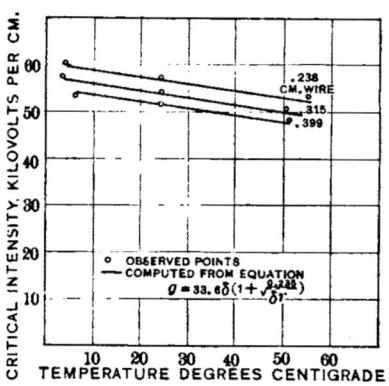

FIG. 10.—VARIATION OF CRITICAL INTENSITY WITH TEMPERATURE AT 76 CM. PRESSURE

Variation of Critical Intensity with Temperature. The curves of Fig. 10 show the variation of critical corona voltage with temperature corrected to the pressure 76 cm. Table III gives the data from which the curves were plotted. The values computed are from the formula

$$g = 33.6\,\delta \left(1 + \frac{0.235}{\sqrt{\delta\, r}}\right)$$

TABLE III

Diameter of conductor	Temp. deg. cent.	Barometer	Test coil volts		Critical intensity	
			Read	Corrected	Obs.	Comp.
0.238	4.0	758	22.6	22.6	60.3	59.8
	24.3	760	21.5	21.5	57.5	56.6
	55.4	754	19.8	20.0	53.5	52.3
0.315	3.7	758	26.4	26.4	57.6	56.8
	24.2	760	25.0	25.0	54.3	53.4
	50.8	754	23.1	23.3	50.7	50.0
0.399	6.3	758	29.1	29.1	53.7	54.2
	24.2	760	28.1	28.1	51.8	51.3
	51.0	754	25.9	26.1	48.1	47.8

The diameter of tube used as outer conductor in these experiments was 10.5 cm. The curves in Fig. 9 are practically straight lines as the range of temperature is not great enough to bring out any curvature. The agreement with the revised Peek equation is also very close here.

Influence of Density of the Medium on Critical Intensity. A simple calculation from the gas equation

$$pv = RT$$

shows that the pressure coefficient and temperature coefficient interpreted in terms of the change in volume of unit mass of gas are the same. In other words the critical corona intensity in air varies nearly as the density whether such change is produced by a change of pressure or temperature. This idea is implicitly stated in Peek's equation in his density factor. It must be remembered, however, that his definition gives only

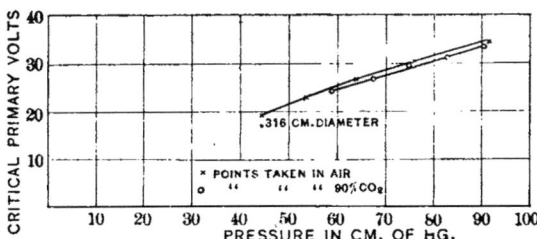

Fig. 11.—Effect of Density of the Medium on Critical Intensity

the relative density. With a view to the more definite investigation of the influence of density as the mass per unit volume we have made some interesting preliminary observations on the corona in a gas heavier than air.

In Fig. 11 are shown two curves of the variation of critical intensity with pressure, one in air and the other in a mixture of carbon dioxide and air, but containing about 90 per cent by volume of the former. Owing to leakage of the tube it was not possible to fill it with the pure gas. It is seen that there is little change due to the presence of the carbon dioxide although its density is about 1.5 times that of air. It appears then from these experiments that the variation of critical intensity does not, in fact, depend on the density, but is rather a function of the separation of the molecules of the gas, since according to the law of Avogadro the number of molecules in a given volume of gas is a function of the pressure and temperature only, and does not depend on the nature of the substance. The indication from these curves then is that the relation of the electric intensity and corona formation is found in the average separation of the molecules. This is in fact a principle tenet of the theory of secondary ionization or ionization by collision as explaining all forms of spark discharge in gases. The opinion has been expressed in several places in this series of papers that the theory of second-

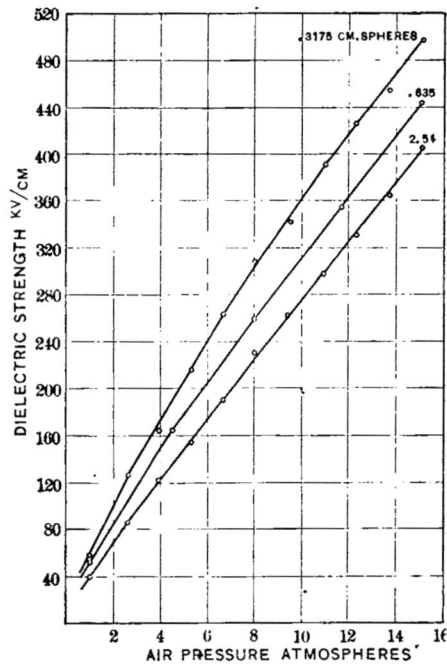

FIG. 12.—SPARKING POTENTIALS BETWEEN SPHERES, BY WATSON

ary ionization offers the most promising explanation of corona formation.

IV. COMPARISON WITH RESULTS ON SPARKING POTENTIALS

Fig. 12 is reproduced from a paper by Watson on "The Dielectric Strength of Air."[6] The curves show the variation of the sparking potentials between spheres with variation of pressure. The pressures range from atmospheric upward so that

---

6. *Jour. Inst. Elec. Engrs.*, Vol. XLIII, 1909.

they are not directly comparable with the pressures in the present set of corona experiments. From the work of other observers, however, it is known that the curves extend down toward the zero until they reach the so-called "critical pressure." Upon further reduction of pressure the curves turn sharply upward. These critical pressures vary with the length of spark gap, ranging from 3 to 0.3 mm. for spark gaps of 1 to 10 mm., respectively.[7]

It is seen by reference to the curves that their general shape is the same as for critical corona intensity. The chief question of interest in both cases is the departure from the linear law as the curvature is probably due to a common cause. By analogy with curves for sparking potentials it may be anticipated that the critical corona intensity may rise at very low pressures. It is well known that it is difficult to get the vacuum tube discharge at very high vacua.

The results obtained with corona in carbon dioxide were to be anticipated from Paschen's law. This law states that the sparking potential depends on the product of the pressure and the spark length. Curves plotted with products of pressure and spark length as abscissas and sparking potentials as ordinates are nearly the same for air and carbon dioxide but differ considerably for hydrogen. No attempt was made to try hydrogen as the medium surrounding the conductor in the present set of experiments owing to the presence of some leakage of the tube which might have resulted in the production of an explosive mixture. We wish to emphasize the simplicity of the corona apparatus as a method for studying the theory of gaseous conduction.

V. Discussion

As most of the observed laws of corona formation are in accord with the theory of ionization by collision, a brief statement of some of the fundamental experiments and conclusions of that theory will not be out of place.

When two parallel conducting plates are connected to a source of potential difference and the gas between them ionized by X-rays or radium, it is found that a current passes. This current increases at first as the potential difference is increased, but later attains a stationary value. No further increase of the current with increasing voltage is noted until a considerably higher voltage is reached when the current again increases rapidly with increasing voltage. The interpretation of this phenomenon is

---

7. "Conduction of Elec. Through Gases," J. J. Thomson, 1906.

that the X-rays produce ions at a definite rate so that the current which can be produced by sweeping out all these ions has a limit. The stationary value of the current spoken of, marks this limit. When, however, the voltage becomes sufficiently high the ions attain a velocity which enables them to produce new ones by collision with neutral atoms. This is known as ionization by collision or secondary ionization. This theory of ionization by collision accounts for the order of magnitude of the critical corona voltage which in the limiting case of plane surfaces is approximately 30 kv. per cm. The mean free path of the electrons is about 6×10^{-5} cm. at 76 cm. pressure and 20 deg. cent. as has been shown by Townsend and others. This is about six times the mean free path of the molecules of the gas. For the ordinary sizes of conductors the voltage over a mean free path of an electron is about 2 volts. This indicates that the critical intensity is that which gives the ionizing voltage of about 10 volts[8] in a distance of five times the mean free path, or in other words some of the electrons having a free path of five or more times the average, start the corona.

The ionization theory fails as yet to show why the critical intensity varies with the size of conductor and why the variation of critical intensity with pressure does not follow a linear law. As has been frequently shown, the critical intensity rises quite rapidly as the size of conductor is reduced. The intensity in the gas falls away as $1/r$ where r is the distance from the center of the conductor, and from this it is seen that the intensity diminishes much more rapidly in the immediate neighborhood of a small conductor than a large one. Nevertheless, the diminution in a distance of five or ten mean free paths of an electron is negligibly small in any practical case.

The corona begins and ends at approximately the same voltage on the e.m.f. wave. This indicates that the rate of recombination of the ions is very great. It appears possible from this fact that the corona will not start until the intensity is high enough over some depth such as half a mm. on account of the great amount of recombination which goes on in the neighboring space, where the intensity is too low.

VI. Conclusions

1. The critical corona-forming electric intensity in air has been determined over the range of pressure from 5 cm. to 108 cm.

---

8. Bishop: *Physical Review*, Vol. XXXIII, 1911.

of mercury, for nine sizes of round conductor of diameters from 0.23 to 0.95 cm.

2. A few observations on the influence of temperature within the range of 5 deg. to 55 deg. cent. are also recorded.

3. The results are in substantial agreement with the empirical relation between electric intensity, pressure and temperature suggested by Peek.

4. Experiments with carbon dioxide indicate that the critical corona intensity is independent of the absolute density of the gas, but depends on the number and spacing of the molecules, in accord with the theory of secondary ionization.

BIBLIOGRAPHY

Steinmetz: *Dielectric Strength of Air*, TRANS. A. I. E. E., Vol. XV, 1898

Scott: *High Voltage Power Transmission*, TRANS. A. I. E. E., Vol. XV, 1898.

Ryan: *Conductivity of Atmosphere at High Voltages*, TRANS. A. I. E. E., Vol. XXIII, 1904.

Mershon: *High Voltage Measurements at Niagara*, TRANS. A. I. E. E., Vol. XXVII, 1908.

Balch: " 80,000-Volt Transmission Line," *Jour. of Elec.*, 1904.

Brecht: " A 500,000-Volt Experimental Line," *Electrotechn. Anzeiger*, Vol. XXVI, 1909.

Lyndon: " The Corona and Design of High Tension Lines," *Elec. Review and Western Electn.*, Vol. LIV, 1909.

Watson: " Atmospheric Loss under Continuous Current," *Electrician*, September 3, 1909; February 11, 18, 1910.

" Dielectric Strength of Compressed Air," *Jour. Inst. Elec. Engr.*, Vol. XLIII, 1909.

Moody and Faccioli: *Experiments on Corona*, TRANS. A. I. E. E., Vol. XXVIII, 1909.

Kemp and Stephens: " Disruptive Voltage in Air," *Inst. Elec. Engr.*, Vol. XLIV, 1910.

Hayden and Steinmetz: *Disruptive Strength of Air*, TRANS. A. I. E. E., Vol. XXIX, 1910.

Whitehead: *The Electric Strength of Air, I, II, III*, TRANS. A. I. E. E., 1910, 1911, 1912.

Peek: *The Law of Corona and the Dielectric Strength of Air, I and II*, TRANS. A. I. E. E., 1911, 1912.

" The Nature of Corona," *G. E. Review*, December, 1912.

Görges, Weidig and Jaensch: " Experiments on Corona Loss," *Electrotechn. Zeitschr.*, 32, 1911.

Wecker: " Sparking Pressure under Commercial Conditions," *Zeitschr. Verins. Deutsch. Eng.*, 55, 1911.

West: *High Voltage Line Loss Tests*, TRANS. A.I.E.E., Vol XXX, 1911.

Faccioli: *Tests of Losses on High Tension Lines*, TRANS. A. I. E. E., 1911.

Zickler: " Zur Berechnung der Koronaverluste," *Electrotechn. und Maschinenbau*, September 15, 1912.

Printed by Libri Plureos GmbH in Hamburg, Germany